Scottish Proverbs

* * *

AN HONEST MAN'S
THE NOBLEST WORK
OF GOD.

Robert Burns
in "The Cotter's Saturday Night"

* * *

Collected by Julie McDonald

More Books

For a complete list of our titles, please write us:
Penfield Press, 215 Brown St., Iowa City, IA 52240

© 1987 by Julie McDonald
All rights reserved. Illustrations and text may not
be reproduced without written approval of Penfield
Press except for a review of the book.
Printed by Julin Printing Co., Monticello, Iowa, on
acid-free paper.
Library of Congress Catalog Number 87-61517
ISBN 0-941016-42-0 paper

The Author

Julie McDonald, related by marriage to the great Clan Donald, is the author of more than a dozen published books, including novels, a biography and a volume of regional history. Her interest in Scottish proverbs began during her research for The Heather and the Rose, a novel based on the adventures and misadventures of Bonnie Prince Charlie and his protectress, Flora Macdonald.

The Calligrapher

Esther Feske was also calligrapher, illustrator and graphic designer for the prize-winning Scandinavian Proverbs by Julie McDonald. Her maternal grandmother was an Oglevie.

The Publishers

John Zug traces his ancestry to the McLelands and the McMahons; Joan Liffring-Zug is a descendant of the Browns of Paisley, Scotland.

Wee Bits

The calligraphic styles in this book are adaptations of 7th-century Insular Half-Uncials and 10th-century Anglo-Saxon Miniscules, both from the manuscript The Lindisfarne Gospels.

Illustrations include the Scottish Lion, a Celtic cross from Iona, a fictional clan badge for the family of Nessie, the Loch Ness monster, and on the cover, a Luckenbooth pin, designed to win the heart of Mary Queen of Scots.

The cover plaid is Black Stewart.

A Wee Explanation

. . .

If you want to know a people, study the proverbs that have evolved from their experience. The bits of folk wisdom I have found while doing research for my novels have delighted me, and so I started collecting them. This book contains distillations of Scottish experience I found while reading for *The Heather and the Rose*. Their tone is quite different from that of the *Scandinavian Proverbs* – sometimes rueful, other times philosophical, occasionally humorous, and always practical.

Robert Burns (1759-1796), the immortal poet of Ayr, wrote many a line that sounds like, and has become, a proverb. It's only fitting that his words should launch each category of this collection.

-Julie McDonald

ROBERT BURNS, the most famous of Scottish poets, was born at Alloway, Ayrshire, on January 25, 1759, a day commemorated annually by Scots all over the world. Born into poverty, Burns sowed the seeds of his untimely death with exhausting labor and inadequate food in his early youth. His amorous appetites were as strong as the vigor of his verse, resulting in memorable love poems. He also spoke for the common man, and his down-to-earth insights have been passed from generation to generation. They have the same enduring verity as the proverbs forged in the hearts of the Scots.

Canny Observations
(Canny: shrewd and cautious in dealing with others.)

* * *

Man's inhumanity to man makes countless thousands mourn.

Robert Burns in "Man Was Made to Mourn"

All bite the bitten dog.

The bairn (child) speaks in
the streets what he heard
by the fireside.

The collie has the brains of a
man and the ways of a woman.

Craft must have clothes,
but truth goes naked.

There's a cure for everything
but stark dead.

The day has eyes;
the night has ears.

He that sleeps with dogs
must rise with fleas.

It's a true dream
that is seen waking.

Trouble follows all extremes.

Fear has long legs.

Long foul, long fair.

Gratitude is a heavy burden.

He who is early up
and has no business
has an ill wife, an ill bed
or an ill conscience.

Nothing comes fairer to light
than what's been long hidden.

Devil speed them that ask
and know full well.

Even a young foot
finds ease in an old slipper.

It's a bare moor you cross
without finding a tuft of heather.

To feed the land before it gets
hungry; to give it rest before
it grows weary; to weed it
well before it gets dirty –
these are the marks of
the good husbandman.

–From the Gaelic

Nearest the king,
     nearest the gallows.

A body lives long after being
     laughed at.

He sits very still
     who has a rip in his trousers.

A day to come seems longer
     than a year that's gone.

Ripe fruit is soonest rotten.

(Precocious children are soonest over the hill.)

"My own property," "My own wife," and "Come home" are the three sweetest sayings in all the world.

–Gaelic proverb

It's dear-cost honey that's licked off a thorn.

No weather's ill if the wind be still.

He that rides behind another cannot saddle when he pleases.

He who never rode never fell.

Concerning
the Almighty

...

They never sought
in vain
that sought
the Lord aright.

Robert Burns in "The Cotter's Saturday Night"

No tear should fall on the face
of a good man dying.

God shapes the back
        for the burden.

God never measures a man
        by inches.

Danger past, God forgotten.

"You have fed me with an
        empty spoon!" (Parishioner's remark to
his clergyman after a poor sermon.)

Friends
and Neighbors

· · ·

If there's another
world,
he lives in bliss;
If there is none,
he made the best
of this.

Robert Burns in "On a Friend"

He that plants trees
loves others besides himself.

Favors unused are favors
abused.

Before you choose a friend,
eat a peck of salt with him.

Friends are lost by calling
often and calling seldom.

He doubles his gift
that gives in time.

It's no loss what a friend gets.

No man can be happy without
a friend nor be sure of a
friend until he's unhappy.

Be slow in choosing a friend
and slower in changing him.

Be a friend to yourself,
   and others will.

To ken (know) a folk,
   you must winter 'em
   and summer 'em.

No man can live longer in
peace than his neighbor pleases.

Lock your door and
   keep your neighbor honest.

The shortest road's
   where the company's good.

human Nature
...
A man's a man for a'that.

Robert Burns in "For A' That and A' That"

The Scotsman is never at home
except when he's abroad.

The Scot will not fight
until he sees his own blood.

When I did well, I heard it never;
when I did ill, I heard it ever.

Do a man a good turn
and he'll never forgive you.

—from the Shetland Islands

He that does you an ill turn
will never forgive you.

He that has a big nose thinks
everybody speaks of it.

The more noble,
the more humble.

He's the slave of a slave
who serves none but himself.

Fools look to tomorrow
    while wise men use tonight.

Wink at small faults,
    for you have big ones yourself.

Love and Marriage

...

The myriad love affairs of Robert Burns gave rise to
lines like these:

But to see her
was to love her,
Love but her,
and love forever.

Robert Burns in "A Fond Kiss"

Follow love and it will flee thee;
Flee love and it will follow thee.

Man is April when he makes
love - December when he is
married.

Married folk are like rats in a
trap - able to get others in
but unable to get
themselves out.

Never marry for money;
ye'll borrow it cheaper.

There belongs more to a bed
than four bare legs.

A bonnie bride is soon dressed;
a short horse is soon curried.

Choose a good mother's daughter,
though her father were the devil.

Fanned fires and forced love
never did well.

Nobody's sweetheart is ugly.

He who tells his wife all
is newly married.

True love's the weft of life,
but sometimes it comes
through a sorrowful shuttle.

The weft is the filling yarn carried across the warp
of a loom by the shuttle.

Money and Property

· · ·

Poor in gear, we're rich in love:

Robert Burns in "The Soldier's Return"

· · ·

O, gie me the lass
that has acres
o'charms,
O, gie me the lass
wi' the weel-stockit*
farms.

Robert Burns in "A Lass Wi' a Tocher" (dowry)

* (well-stocked)

Mickle (much) would always
                    have more.

Content is no child of wealth.

An empty pocket
goes quickly through the market.

Always take the fee
    when the tear's in the eye.

A man has no more goods
    than he gets good of.

Put two pennies in a purse,
    and they'll creep together.

He knows not the pleasures of
    plenty who never felt the
    pains of poverty.

A shroud has no pockets.

The purse of a sick person
prolongs his care.

Those who need credit most
get it least.

Never ask for more
than you can make good use of.

Bear wealth well,
and poverty will bear itself.

Liked is half-bought.

Few possessions, few cares.

Sage Advice

...

But still
keep something
to yoursel'
Ye scarcely tell
to ony (anyone).

Robert Burns in "Epistle to a Young Friend"

Eat your fill but pocket none
        is gardener's law.

Do not tell your foe
        when your foot sleeps.

Nothing should be done in
    haste but catching fleas.

Never draw your dirk (knife)
    when a blow will do it.

Charity begins at home
    but should not end there.

You can beguile none
    but those that trust in you.

Be the thing
    that you would be called.

We must not wish the burn
    (stream) dry because it wets
    our feet.

If you don't see the bottom,
                    don't wade.

The devil is always good
                    to beginners.

Keep your tongue a prisoner,
    and your body will go free.

Give your tongue more holidays
    than your head.

Let him that's cold blow the fire.

Wait for dead men's shoes,
    and you'll long be barefoot.

He that tholes (bears) overcomes.

He that has a good crop
    may endure some thistles.

Food and Drink

...

The halesome
        parritch
(wholesome porridge)
Chief of Scotia's food.

Robert Burns in "The Cotter's Saturday Night"

...

Inspiring bold,
    John Barleycorn,
what dangers thou
canst make us scorn!

Robert Burns in "Tam o'Shanter."

Come uncalled, sit unserved.

Deal small and serve all.

Bread is the staff of life,
but pudding makes
a good crutch.

The bait must be gathered
when the tide's out.

All's lost that's put in a
broken dish. (May be taken literally or as
favors done for an ungrateful person.)

Boil stones in butter,
and the broth will be good.

A broken bannock
(cake made of coarse meal)
is as good as eaten.

He that buys land buys stones,
he that buys beef buys bones,
he that buys nuts buys shells,
he that buys good ale
      buys nothing else.